MONEY ADVICE AND DEBT COUNSELLING

D1341313

The Policy Studies Institute (PSI) is Britain's leading independent research organisation undertaking studies of economic, industrial and social policy, and the workings of political institutions.

PSI is a registered charity, run on a non-profit basis, and is not associated with any political party, pressure group or commercial interest.

PSI attaches great importance to covering a wide range of subject areas with its multi-disciplinary approach. The Institute's researchers are organised in groups which currently cover the following programmes:

Crime, Justice and Youth Studies – *Employment and Society* – *Ethnic Equality and Diversity* – *European Industrial Development* – *Family Finances* – *Information and Citizenship* – *Information and Cultural Studies* – *Social Care and Health Studies* – *Work, Benefits and Social Participation*

This publication arises from the Family Finances group and is one of over 30 publications made available by the Institute each year.

Information about the work of PSI, and a catalogue of available books can be obtained from:

Marketing Department, PSI
100 Park Village East, London NW1 3SR

Money Advice and Debt Counselling

Elaine Kempson

POLICY STUDIES INSTITUTE
London

The publishing imprint of the independent
POLICY STUDIES INSTITUTE
100 Park Village East, London NW1 3SR
Telephone: 0171-387 2171 Fax: 0171-388 0914

ISBN 0 85374 652 4

PSI Research Report 797

A CIP catalogue record of this book is available from the British Library.

1 2 3 4 5 6 7 8 9

PSI publications are available from
BEBC Distribution Ltd
P O Box 1496, Poole, Dorset, BH12 3YD

Books will normally be despatched within 24 hours. Cheques should be made payable to BEBC Distribution Ltd.

Credit card and telephone/fax orders may be placed on the following freephone numbers:

FREEPHONE: 0800 262260
FREEFAX: 0800 262266

Booktrade representation (UK & Eire):
Broadcast Books
24 De Montfort Road, London SW16 1LW
Telephone: 0181-677 5129

PSI subscriptions are available from PSI's subscription agent
Carfax Publishing Company Ltd
P O Box 25, Abingdon, Oxford OX14 3UE

Laserset by Policy Studies Institute
Printed in Great Britain by Bourne Press, Bournemouth, BH1 4QA

Contents

Ackowledgements

A number of people have given me invaluable assistance in preparing this report. In particular, I should like to thank staff at the Money Advice Assoiation, National Association of Citizens Advice Bureaux, Federation of Independent Advice Centres, National Debtline, and the Money Advice Trust. They provided me with useful information which has been incorporated into the report and have read and commented upon earlier drafts. Finally I should like to acknowledge the financial support we received from the Department of Social Security which has enabled me to carry out the review.

1 Introduction

The first money advice service, offering debt counselling and case work to individuals in debt, was set up by Birmingham Settlement in the early 1970s. Since then a large number of services have been established across the country using a variety of methods to help those with financial problems.

This report was commissioned by the Department of Social Security to provide an up to date assessment of the provision of money advice and debt counselling in Britain. It begins by drawing together information on the scope and nature of existing provision, looks at the resources and support available to those providing money advice and finally evaluates the most effective and efficient methods of delivering this service.

The study is mainly based on a review of published research and other reports that were available. We have also gathered information directly from key organisations involved in money advice and are very grateful for the assistance given by the Birmingham Settlement, the Federation of Independent Advice Centres; the Money Advice Association; the Money Advice Trust the National Association of Citizens Advice Bureaux and the National Consumer Council.

2 The Development of Money Advice

The first specialist money advice centre in Britain was set up in 1971 by the Birmingham Settlement. Solicitors who operated the legal advice and assistance scheme at the Settlement were identifying an increasing number of people who needed specialist, time consuming, financial advice. To meet this need the Settlement employed a small team of money advisers who concentrated on helping people who were in multiple debt. They advised clients with debt problems, negotiated with creditors to achieve a fair level of repayment and, if necessary, represented the debtor in any court action. The service was intended to cover the whole of the West Midlands and operated at first from the Settlement in the Aston area of Birmingham and later through an additional money advice centre in Birmingham city centre. They did not, then, get many enquiries direct from the public but mainly received referrals from other agencies: citizens advice bureaux, social services, courts and other advice centres.

Also in 1971, a probation officer was appointed as a part-time welfare officer at Birmingham County Court, to assist debtors in the presentation of their cases. This post became full-time in 1973 and was subsequently transferred to the citizens advice bureau.

Growth in money advice provision was initially slow. By 1977, when the National Consumer Council carried out the first overview of advice provision, there was only one further specialist money advice centre – in Liverpool. This had been set up in 1974 and at that stage had 'a heavy bias towards welfare rights problems'. In addition the National Consumer Council identified approximately 100 citizens advice bureaux who were providing regular financial advice sessions staffed by volunteer accountants. These CAB sessions were not really money advice services as we have come to know them. The main enquiries they dealt with were taxation, consumer credit, mortgages and family budgeting (National Consumer Council 1977).

By the early 1980s, the deepening recession and rapid rise in unemployment led to an increased demand for money advice and acted as a spur to further development of services. So that, in 1982, the National Consumer Council identified 15 specialist money advice services in Britain which, between them, ran 19 money advice centres (National Consumer Council 1982).

Shortly after this report, in 1984, there were two important developments at a national level, which were to act as a further spur to the development of money advice. First, agencies specialising in money advice and debt counselling, with assistance from the National Consumer Council, set up the Money Advice Association. The aims of this new Association were:

- to promote the development of money advice and education in money matters;

- to provide a forum for exchange of views, information and experience in the field;

- to encourage the provision of training and support for those working in the field;

- to exercise a responsible influence on the development of policies affecting the financial interests of consumers, both locally and nationally;

- to carry out or support such other activities as may be in accord with the above objectives.

Secondly, the National Association of Citizens Advice Bureaux founded the Money Advice Project Group to develop the provision of specialist money advice and support for those giving advice across the CAB network.

The long-term effects of the recession, coupled with a concern about the rising use of consumer credit, acted as a further impetus, and money advice provision began to pick up markedly. So that, in mid 1986, the Policy Studies Institute identified 100 money advice services, including both money advice centres and individual money advisers working within citizens advice bureaux and local authority departments (Hinton and Berthoud 1988).

The most comprehensive review of money advice provision, commissioned by the National Consumer Council in 1989, succeeded in tracking down 221 voluntary organisations with specialist money advice staff and a further 40 services provided by local authorities. These included:

- 16 money advice centres, specialising in money advice casework;
- 20 money advice support units, providing training and consultancy services to other agencies;
- 196 money advisers working from advice agencies;
- 29 money advisers attached to local authority departments – mostly in housing departments, but including some in consumer protection or social services and even in the treasurers department.

Current levels of provision
Repeating this review was beyond both the timescale and budget of the present study. Instead we have had to rely on a range of sources to attempt to up-date the 1989 National Consumer Council review. These sources have included the records of the Money Advice Association, Money Advice Scotland, the National Association of Citizens Advice Bureaux (NACAB), the Federation of Independent Advice Centres (FIAC) as well as a new directory of money advice services (Brady and O'Brien 1994).

Together these suggest that money advice provision has continued to expand, almost certainly fuelled by the most recent recession and debt crisis. Compared to the early years of money advice, provision is now available through a wide diversity of organisations.

Specialist money advice centres
The number of specialist money advice centres has not grown at anything like the rate of other forms of provision and is little greater now than it was at the time of the 1989 review. Exact numbers are difficult to assess but there are probably no more than 20 (Brady and O'Brien 1994, Money Advice Scotland 1991). Most development has been through existing organisations employing specialist money advice workers.

Money advisers in other independent advice centres
NACAB was able to identify from its current database 196 citizens advice bureaux in England and Wales where staff spent more than 15 hours a week on money advice. Across the CAB network levels of money advice provision varied widely: some bureaux recorded no

time at all while others had the equivalent of three or four full-time workers. 192 CABx in England and Wales are currently affiliated to the Money Advice Association – two-fifths of the members of the Association – and a further 46 Scottish CABx are affiliated to Money Advice Scotland.

The other major network of independent advice centres is the Federation of Independent Advice Centres. Of the 986 advice centres who are members of FIAC, 562 (57 per cent) said that they covered money advice, although we do not know the extent of this work in each case. In addition a further 24 independent advice centres in Scotland have specialist money advisers (Money Advice Scotland 1991).

In addition to these two large networks of local advice agencies, ten of the 59 law centres in the United Kingdom offer a specialist debt counselling service, and many of the others handle repossession cases. Indeed, law centres generally play an active role in duty rota schemes at the County Courts. Similarly, Shelter housing aid centres and SHAC undertake cases involving either rent or mortgage arrears (Brady and O'Brien 1994, Money Advice Scotland 1991).

Money advice support units
There are currently about 21 money advice support units in the United Kingdom, whose primary role is the provision of training and consultancy services for the money advisers working in other independent advice centres. But, in addition to these, there are approximately another 10 organisations that offer a front-line money advice centre as well as specialising in providing support and back-up to money advisers working in other agencies (Brady and O'Brien 1994, Money Advice Scotland 1991).

Local authorities
Besides providing funds to independent advice centres, local authorities contribute to money advice provision in two ways: some run specialist money advice centres, but more commonly they employ money advisers within individual local authority departments. Some 54 local authorities currently offer money advice services (Brady and O'Brien 1994, Money Advice Scotland 1991). This provision is in part a response to the growing numbers of people in poverty and debt generally, particularly within large urban local authorities, but it is also

likely to have arisen through concern about debts owed to local authorities themselves – rent, poll tax and council tax arrears (Wainwright, Ford and Doling 1992).

A range of different local authority departments are involved with the direct provision of money advice, reflecting these two possible motivations. The main providers are trading standards, social services (especially welfare rights departments) and housing departments, although a small number of finance and treasurers' departments also employ money advisers (Brady and O'Brien 1994, Money Advice Scotland 1991).

One of the first money advisers was employed by a probation service and, although that service was subsequently handed over to the local CAB, eight local probation services have recently been identified as providing money advice and they are one of the growth areas for membership of the Money Advice Association (Brady and O'Brien 1994).

Creditors

The 1990s have seen the involvement of commercial creditor organisations in the direct provision of money advice. Most notably these are banks and building societies who have faced increasing numbers of their customers falling into mortgage arrears.

The Woolwich Building Society set up the first telephone helpline for customers with mortgage arrears in 1992, since when a number of others have created similar services. Precise figures are difficult to come by, but by piecing together all the available information we were able to identify twelve creditors who were offering helplines and self-help packs to their customers. Two organisations have gone further still.

The Portman Building Society has created a subsidiary, Ridgeway Financial Services, that provides general money advice but whose primary concern is, nevertheless, recovering arrears owed to the Society.

The only fully independent money advice service that operates as a subsidiary of a commercial creditor was set up by Mortgage Express. The service has recruited a skilled adviser from Birmingham Settlement and offers a comprehensive money advice service, including home visits to clients who require them.

In addition to these services offered by individual creditors, in March 1993, a number of creditors contributed to a new project to set up the West Yorkshire Consumer Credit Counselling Service in Leeds. The service was inspired by the American model of money advice (and the service operated in Houston in particular), whereby the service is funded out of a voluntary commission paid by creditors of 15 per cent of any debts repaid to them.

Self-help groups and charities

One of the most recent areas of money advice development has taken place through national charities. In fact, the Money Advice Association identified this as the largest area of growth in their membership in recent months. It would seem that two types of charity have been drawn to money advice provision: benevolent societies and charities that provide information and support to particular groups of people.

The benevolent societies – organisations like the Soldiers, Sailors and Air Forcemen's Association – found that demands being made on their funds outstripped the money they had available and they have responded by setting up debt advice services.

Similarly, student unions and health-related charities, like the Parkinsons Disease Society, are increasingly coming into contact with people who are getting into debt. They, too, have responded by training staff in debt counselling.

Geographical coverage

Despite the growth in the overall numbers of agencies giving money advice, access varies enormously from one part of the country to another. Like all advice services, money advice centres have tended to be located in urban areas, and inner cities in particular, with rural areas often very poorly served. At the same time the regional development of money advice has followed the areas worst hit by earlier recessions. The West Midlands, Greater Manchester and Strathclyde have fairly extensive provision, while Wales, the South West and even the South East have much poorer levels of provision.

These disparities of provision seem to have come about as a result of two influences. First, local authorities were not subject to such tight financial constraints during the recession at the beginning of the 1980s as they have been during the more recent recession. Consequently

7

those affected by the debt problem earlier were better able to respond by funding money advice either in the voluntary sector or through their own departments. Secondly, Labour-controlled local authorities have always provided greater levels of funding for advice services than Conservative-controlled ones. In part this is because levels of need for advice are greater in Labour-voting areas, but it is not the whole explanation.

The range of approaches to money advice provision

The development of money advice has been characterised not only by the diversity of organisations involved but also by the range of approaches to the delivery of money advice.

One-to-one counselling

The traditional approach for money advice is based on one-to-one counselling of people in multiple debt. Typically, money advisers begin with a lengthy initial interview during which they attempt to collect a full picture of clients' finances. Money advisers then use a three pronged approach involving maximising clients' income, minimising their outgoings and then preparing a full financial statement of their income and expenditure as a basis for negotiation with their creditors.

Following its conference in the Spring of 1989, the Money Advice Liaison Group (then comprising the National Association of Citizens Advice Bureaux, Money Advice Association, Money Advice Scotland, Birmingham Settlement, Consumer Credit Trade Association and the Retail Credit Group) set up a working party to review the whole question of financial statements. The working party, which was made up of representatives from both the credit industry and money advice, evolved a standard financial statement for use in negotiating repayment arrangements with non-priority creditors. Although the use of financial statements is common in money advice work, the model piloted by the Group has not been accepted in the way that had been hoped.

The early money advice services often provided a 'customer account' facility, whereby clients made a regular payment to the money advice service, who then arranged for that money to be allocated to the various creditors owed money. As services proliferated, most were unable to offer this facility because of the costs involved. Moreover, there was a continuing debate about the relative advantages of managing clients money for them as opposed to helping them to do so for themselves.

But two developments have put the whole question of client accounts back onto the agenda. The first of these is the West Yorkshire Consumer Credit Counselling Service (WYCCCS). Like other debt counsellors, staff at the WYCCCS draw up a detailed statement of income and expenditure for all their clients and prepare a schedule of repayments covering all creditors. They not only provide a facility for managing those repayments, but will, in time, derive their funding in the form of commission on the money repaid. The plans to expand the WYCCCS to a national network of services whilst keeping the West Yorkshire centre as the central support office, managing payment plans on behalf of other licensed agencies.

This approach has always received a guarded response by the money advice movement since it is based on the premise that, between them, clients will be able to repay sufficient money to keep the service operating. While there will be clients who have a reasonable income, but have over-committed themselves, these people do not (as we shall see in detail in the next chapter) represent a large proportion of money advice clients. This is widely acknowledged by those who have been instrumental in setting up the WYCCCS, who see themselves as meeting the needs of a particular group of people that they perceive to have been poorly served by money advice services in the past. (Consumer Credit Assocation News January 1994, London Money Advice Support Unit 1993). At the same time, it has been estimated that for the service to be viable financially only 30 per cent of the clients will need to be able to start repaying their arrears immediately. Where clients are judged to be unable to meet their commitments the staff of WYCCCS will negotiate write-offs with their creditors.

The other significant development is the proposed Instalments Payment Plan Facility (IPPF), which is to be piloted in Scotland in late 1994. IPPF will be administered by the 'Paylink Trust' comprising representatives of the credit industry and money advice as well as Revenue Management Services Ltd, which is part of the Legal and Trade Financial Services Group. It has long been acknowledged that many clients of money advice centres live on such low incomes that they can often afford only minimal offers of repayment. This incurs high costs both for the creditors who need to process the payments and for the clients who must often pay charges to post offices or banks to make the payments on their behalf. IPPF will reduce both these costs by offering a free payment facility to money advice clients and holding payments on behalf of creditors until an agreed minimum level of dividend has been accumulated. The scheme, which will be non-profit-making, will be funded through a commission deducted from the amount repaid to creditors. The early signs are that money advisers view the proposals with some interest (Bassano 1993, Conlin 1994).

Money advisers have, however, become aware of the limitations of one-to-one debt counselling as a way of providing money advice. First, clients tend to contact money advice centres only when arrears have reached a very serious and complex level. Secondly, and partly as a result of this, personal counselling can be very time consuming and costly. Resolving an individual case takes an average of 18 hours of adviser time (Money Advice Funding Working Party, 1990) Personal counselling also requires the client to attend a money advice centre and for many of those in debt this may not be possible.

This awareness encouraged money advisers to develop other ways of providing money advice, aiming to provide clients with assistance at an earlier stage of arrears and so avoiding the need for such a high degree of staff involvement and intervention.

Telephone helplines
A number of money advice services have set up special telephone helplines in an attempt to contact clients before they get into multiple arrears. This is also one of the main areas where creditors themselves have set up their own money advice initiatives. But, without doubt, the largest and best-funded is National Debtline based at the Birmingham Settlement. The helpline was originally founded in 1987 as Housing Debtline, to prevent homelessness caused by mortgage and rent arrears. Unlike other helplines, however, it covered the whole of England and Wales, not just a particular locality.

It soon became clear that there was a great deal of demand for a telephone advice service covering debts more generally and in 1988 the helpline was re-launched as National Debtline. Surveys of callers demonstrate that, as hoped, National Debtline clients are making contact at an earlier stage of arrears than are those who use the one-to-one counselling services – commonly they ring the Debtline within two months of falling behind on any payments (National Debtline 1992, Johnson 1993).

Callers to telephone helplines are assisted in one of two ways. They can be given basic advice and then put in touch with their nearest money advice service. Or, perhaps more commonly, they are provided with advice and guidance on how to negotiate with creditors or how to make representations at court hearings themselves.

Self-help packs

Staff at Housing Debtline, and later National Debtline, developed detailed self-help packs that could be sent to clients following their telephone call to the service. The packs, *Dealing with your debts* (one for tenants and the other for home owners), contain detailed information and advice that clients need to draw up a personal budget which can be used to produce a financial statement. They then guide clients through negotiations for priority and other debts as well as how to cope with court procedures (National Debtline 1993a and 1993b).

While there will always be clients who need practical assistance from a money adviser, a survey carried out by National Debtline (as we shall see in detail later) suggested that self-help packs can be an effective way of providing money advice to large numbers of people. The survey indicated that 71 per cent of clients using the pack had successfully negotiated payment plans with at least some of their creditors (National Debtline 1992).

Although these packs were originally developed to be used in conjunction with telephone counselling, increasingly they are being used to complement face-to-face advice given in generalist advice agencies. The arguments in favour of this approach are two-fold. First, by working out their own financial statements, clients can retain a greater degree of control over their budgets. Secondly, it is claimed that up to 60 per cent of casework time can be saved by giving clients a self-help pack costing just £1 (Money Advice Trust 1993).

The National Debtline packs have provided the source material for self-help packs prepared by other organisations, including creditors. There have been a number of local initiatives, but the main national one was funded at the National Association of Citizens Advice Bureaux by the National Westminster Bank. Drawing on the experience of National Debtline, this resulted in a model self-help pack, which has been adapted on a regional basis to tailor information to the practices of local creditors and utilities.

The effectiveness of these packs was monitored by NACAB, looking at them from the enquirers', CAB advisers' and creditors' points of view. All three groups found the packs comprehensive, clearly written and helpful, but there was some difference of opinion about *how* they should be used. The advisers tended to view them as a useful adjunct to face-to-face advice and long-term support. This approach was characterised 'supported self-help', as enquirers were not given a booklet without an interview having first taken place. Enquirers, however, found the booklets gave them confidence in their dealing with creditors and that the response of creditors often altered significantly in favour of the client when it was clear that they knew what they were doing. This was in marked contrast to the response they had received when they had tried to sort things out before contacting the CAB and suggests that 'unsupported self-help' could well have been successful in a number of cases. Creditors preferred a self-help approach to dealing through an intermediary for two main reasons. First they felt that it made people take responsibility for their debts and secondly, they preferred dealing directly with customers since it was quicker and easier to reach an agreement (Wann 1993, Wann 1994).

Taken together this evidence suggests that self-help packs can help a number of people to resolve debt problems with their creditors without the need for practical assistance from a money adviser. There are, however, cases where a self-help approach alone is likely to be inadequate – particularly when an enquirer has multiple debts. But even in these cases self-help packs can be a valuable adjunct to a casework approach, with adviser and enquirer working together to sort out complex debt problems.

Outreach work
Many money advice centres and local authorities have decided that a more active, outreach approach to money advice offers a better chance of contacting clients before they get into multiple debt. This has been achieved in two different ways: establishing advice surgeries based in local neighbourhoods and employing outreach workers who make contact with people believed to be getting into difficulties.

To give just one example from the independent advice sector, Birmingham Settlement has now withdrawn from its involvement in the Birmingham city centre money advice unit. Instead, resources have been concentrated on supporting outreach surgeries in known areas of poverty such as Sparkbrook and Winson Green. The Settlement also has plans to raise funding for a black outreach worker to be placed in the local advice centre in Aston, addressing the particular needs of the local Pakistani and Bangladeshi community.

Local authority welfare rights teams have often provided benefits advice sessions on housing estates and in areas without easy access to other advice services. It was a natural development of their service to begin offering money advice in the same way, since so many of their clients were drawn from the groups at highest risk of debt.

At the same time, local authority housing departments, concerned about mounting rent arrears, appointed money advisers. Many of these advisers work closely with the rent collection staff, making contact with tenants known to be falling into arrears, but offering them general money advice and debt counselling in much the same way as other money advisers.

Court based services

One of the earliest money advice services was, as we have seen, a worker (now employed by the CAB) who was attached to the County Court in Birmingham. A similar service has since been set up by the CAB at Liverpool County Court and there is also a citizens advice bureau at the Royal Courts of Justice which employs a money adviser.

The main area of development has, however, been in duty rota schemes, 32 of which are held at county courts. Typically they concentrate on identifying and assisting people who are attending housing possession hearings and were set up because of concern that people were losing their homes with minimal court hearings – often lasting just a few minutes. These schemes are generally run collaboratively by staff from a number of advice agencies and may, also, include private practice solicitors. (National Consumer Council 1992).

Business Debtline

A recent innovation in money advice provision was the extension of services to cover small business debt. The problems faced by self-employed people are frequently far more complex than they are for people facing personal debt alone. Often their personal and business finances are indistinguishable, with their homes used as security for business loans. In addition to the normal range of priority creditors they may owe money to the Inland Revenue and to Customs and Excise for VAT payments. The recent recession has had a large effect on the survival of small businesses and increasing numbers of people facing small business failure have been turning to money advice services for assistance.

Recognising that this area of work called for staff with specialist knowledge and skills, Birmingham Settlement set up *Business Debtline* in October 1992. This has six full-time equivalent staff including a lawyer, a former tax inspector, a banker on secondment and two generalist money advisers. They also work closely with two local insolvency practitioners. The service is delivered in three ways, mirroring general practice within the Settlement – a telephone helpline, self-help packs and one-to-one counselling. The service is currently targeted on Birmingham but, with 40 per cent of enquiries from the West Midlands and beyond, there is a clear need for the development of a national service. Business Debtline is now planning to offer franchises to other organisations wishing to set up similar services, which is seen as the best way to achieve this aim.

Summary

Since the first money advice services were set up in 1971 there has been a substantial growth in the numbers and range of organisations offering money advice. There are now at least 500 organisations that offer specialist money advice and, while independent advice services are still in the majority, they include local authorities, commercial creditors and national charities. We look in more detail at the resources for money advice, and the adequacy of those resources, in the next chapter.

Alongside this growth in numbers, there has been a diversification in styles of work. The traditional style of one-to-one counselling still probably predominates, but many services now offer telephone helplines, self-help packs and outreach services. We return to a consideration of the effectiveness of these different styles of work in Chapter 4.

3 Resources and Support for Money Advice

Money advice provision cannot be judged solely in terms of the numbers of organisations offering services. To get a clearer picture of the adequacy of current provision we need to look in more detail at the resources deployed for those services – including both the levels of funding and the numbers of skilled money advisers. We need also to consider the infra-structure that supports the work of front-line money advisers: the training courses, information materials, consultancy services and mechanisms for co-ordination and liaison between agencies.

Funding

Despite several attempts to collect the information, there is no comprehensive up-to-date picture of the levels of funding for money advice services. A report, commissioned by the Money Advice Trust estimated that about £12 million a year is spent on money advice in England and Wales, with a further £3 million in Scotland (Money Advice Trust 1993). This is, however, something of an overestimate, since it includes the annual grants made each year to the National Association of Citizens Advice Bureaux and its Scottish equivalent, Citizens Advice Scotland. These grants are given by central government to enable these two organisations to run headquarters offices to support the CAB network generally. While a part of this money is, undoubtedly, used to support money advice services it is nowhere near the total funding that these two organisations receive in grant-aid each year.

A more realistic figure can be calculated from the review of advice services conducted for the National Consumer Council in 1990. Allowing for non-response to their questionnaire it would seem that about £3 million was being spent on money advice in the United Kingdom at that time. About a third of this money was spent by local authorities on services which they provided themselves, the remaining two-thirds funded money advice in the independent sector (National Consumer Council 1990). This was allocated across the main types of service provision in the following way.

- Specialist money advice centres
  - independent sector £384,000
  - local local authority sector £485,000
- Money advice support units £774,000
- Money advisers within independent advice centres
  - generalist agencies £686,000
  - law centres and specialist advice agencies £93,000
- Money advice workers in local authority departments £598,000

Reworking these figures, the Money Advice Working Party calculated the percentage of total funding of independent money advice services provided by different bodies. The figures are given in Table 1 below.

Table 1   Sources of funding for independent money advice services

	Column percentages
Local authority grant aid	50
Urban Programme	19
NACAB/local authority partnerships	7
Community Programme	1
Charitable trusts	4
Private sector	16
Other	3

Source: Money Advice Funding Working Party, 1990

It was clear from these figures that funding came from three main sources, and these continue to be the main funders of money advice.

- *Local authorities,* either in the form of grant-aid to independent advice services or direct funding of services provided by local authorities themselves.

- *Central government,* again through grant-aid, mostly through the Urban Programme fund, but also on a case-by-case basis through the legal aid scheme.

- *Creditor organisations,* through grant-aid to independent advice services; direct funding of services provided by creditors themselves, and, most recently, funding provided as a proportion of debts repaid.

Local authorities

Traditionally, the largest share of funding, especially for front-line money advice, has been provided by local authorities. In 1990 they contributed about £1 million for services they provided directly them-selves and at least a further £1 million (half of the total) towards the running costs of money advice services in the independent sector. On top of this there were local authority contributions to the Urban Programme funded projects and those set up on partnership funding with NACAB.

Although it remains the principle source of funding, control of local authority spending by central government, leading to capping at the extreme, has meant that many advice agencies find this source of funding increasingly precarious.

Central government

In 1990, the main source of central government funding was through its Urban Programme, which then provided about a fifth of all the money to independent money advice services. Funding from central goverment has, however, fallen away quite considerably as the Urban Programme has been curtailed, leaving local authorities to pick up much more of the bill for money advice.

The other main source of central goverment funding comes through the legal aid scheme, which is currently restricted to organisations employing a qualified lawyer. Demand for assistance through this scheme has been growing steadily in recent years. In 1992-3 105,000 'HP and debt' cases were paid for under the legal advice and assistance (green form) part of the legal aid scheme (Legal Aid 1993). Although many of these will have been submitted by private practice solicitors, a substantial number would have come from independent money advice services run by organisations like law centres, the Mary Ward Centre and Birmingham Settlement, that employ qualified lawyers.

The only money advice service that has received direct funding from government was Birmingham Settlement, which in 1987 received £32,000 a year year in grant aid from the Department of the Environment for Housing Debtline. But, in 1990, this came to an end and the shortfall in funding was met by the Retail Credit Group.

Creditors

Cut backs in local authority and central goverment funding, together with a growing belief that creditor organisations should shoulder some of the bill for providing money advice, has turned the focus of the funding debate to the private sector. In 1988 a committee was set up, chaired by Lord Ezra, to consider the future funding for money advice. The committee identified £365,900 of private funding for independent money advice plus an additional £250,000 grant from NatWest for the National Association of Citizens Advice Bureaux (NACAB) to provide money advice training over a three year period. They estimated that there was then a total future commitment of £2.5 million from the private sector for the years 1989-1992 (Money Advice Funding Working Pary 1990).

The committee recommended the foundation of a charitable trust to 'receive, disburse and monitor private sector funding of money advice'. Its target was to increase funding to a total of £6 million over a three year period (Money Advice Funding Working Party 1990).

As a direct result of the committee's report, the Money Advice Trust was established with the aim of stimulating and channelling increased funding from private sector organisations. Initial optimism has, however, proved only partially founded. The Trust has failed to achieve anything like the impact on funding that had been hoped.

Between July 1990 and December 1992 the Trust raised only £480,000 (Money Advice Trust, 1993). But, in addition, the Trust had arranged staff secondments to money advice services from the credit industry to the equivalent value of £450,000 (National Consumer Council 1992). There are a number of explanations for this shortfall.

The Trust was launched just as the credit industry faced rising levels of bad debt. These partly arose as a consequence of high interest rates at a time when households had very heavy mortgage and credit commitments. And, in part, they were due to the onset of recession which led to widespread redundancy among white collar workers in the South of England as well as the more traditional victims of recession among blue collar workers and households in the Midlands and North of the country. The net result was that few creditors had spare cash that they could give to help develop independent money advice. Where money was available it was often spent by creditors to improve their own services to the people who owed them money.

The other possible reason for the difficulties the Trust faced is a more technical one. In approaching individual creditor organisations the Trust suggested a level of donation that was based on their total outstanding loans, so that the contributions that were requested from some sections of the credit industry (most notably the mortgage lenders) were disproportionate to the numbers of their customers who were in default and might need the assistance of a money adviser.

Finally, there was a structural problem. Although it was always hoped that the Money Advice Trust would become the main channel for funding from the credit industry to money advice services, it had no mechanism to ensure this. Whilst there were some notable fund-raising successes, a number of creditors continued to fund money advice services direct, rather than through a central Trust fund. So that, for example, Nat West provided funding to the National Association of Citizens Advice Bureaux, the Retail Credit Group contributed to the running costs of National Debtline and a number of money advice support units received direct funding from private sector organisations.

Funds raised by the Money Advice Trust have formed only a small part of the estimated total £1.4 million current contributions from the private sector and independent money advice continues to be heavily dependent on a range of sources for funding.

In its first year, 1992, the Trust made a total of seven grants totalling £173,000, mostly to either national or regional organisations, with the largest single sum going to the NACAB Greater Manchester Money Advice Support Unit (Table 2).

During 1993, just under £140,000 was given in grant aid but another £130,000 had already been committed – most of it going to the same agencies as had been funded the previous year. National Debtline received the largest grant from the Trust to aid the expansion of the telephone counselling service. A further grant will be made in 1994/5 towards funding of NACAB money advice support units.

Table 2   Money Advice Trust, Grants made during 1992 and 1993

	1993 £	1992 £
Grants made		
Birmingham Settlement, National Debtline	64,600	42,000
NACAB Greater Manchester MASU	40,000	74,691
Money Advice Scotland	8,000	
Money Advice Association	10,464	16,605
NACAB, South East MASU	14,400	20,000
Broadcast Support Services, Moneyfax	-	5,000
Citizens Advice Scotland, Edinbury MASU	-	6,640
Norfolk Money Advice	9,290	-
	138,754	172,936
Grants which had been committed but not paid at 31 December 1993		
Birmingham Settlement, National Debtline	118,000	
Northern Ireland Association of CABx	7,500	
BBC Moneyfax	5,000	
	130,500	

Source: Money Advice Trust, Accounts for 1993

Most recently, some sections of the credit industry have decided to make funding available for the Registry Trust initiative, the West Yorkshire Consumer Credit Counselling Service based in Leeds. The funding of this service follows a pattern well-established in the United States, but until now resisted by money advisers in the voluntary sector. Initial start-up grants have been provided for the WYCCCS that will, eventually, be self-financing. After raising £300,000 from the credit industry to start the service, the intention is that creditor organisations will agree to return 15 per cent of the money repaid by debtors assisted by the centre to meet the service's running costs. Plans to develop a network of Consumer Credit Counselling Services are now well established and a further £300,000 has been committed towards the estimated £1.5 million it will take to establish the network.

The continuing difficulties raising funds from the private sector, has renewed calls for a statutory levy on the consumer credit industry, both from independent money advisers and from others in the consumer lobby.

Concern about the long-term funding for money advice services led the National Consumer Council to publish a consultation paper on the options for funding money advice services through a statutory levy. Responses were received from almost 70 organisations including money advisers, local and central government and the credit industry. The consultation showed that there was no consensus about the case for a statutory levy. Some respondents felt that 'the causes of over-indebtedness are not just the responsibility of the credit industry'. Others felt that lenders had 'wider social responsibilities towards the casualties of credit which should be reflected in their contributions towards the funding of money advice services'. The Money Advice Trust did not consider that a statutory duty was appropriate 'at this stage' preferring instead a system based on voluntary contributions. But it did conclude that, if this were the only option, then it would support the introduction of a statutory levy (National Consumer Council 1992b).

Recognising the difference of opinion that existed, the NCC considered that the debate about funding was 'too important to leave to the credit industry and money advisers'. Although they did not recommend the introduction of a statutory levy, they felt there was potential for improving the funding for money advice services, with central government taking a more active role. They favoured a 'mixed model of funding' with the Department of Trade and Industry assuming responsibility for this. More specifically, they recommended that the DTI should:

- find ways of encouraging voluntary contributions from the credit industry;

- identify ways of making a voluntary levy more effective by considering more even handed ways of raising money than the proportion of outstandings proposed earlier by the Money Advice Trust;

- commission research on the most effective way of delivering money advice services;

- • explore the possibility for linking the funding of money advice to debt recovery as in the United States (and subsequently developed by the WYCCS);

- • ensure that local authorities are able to continue funding local money advice services by recognising the funding commitments through the central grant allocation (National Consumer Council 1992c).

Staffing

There are no accurate up-to-date figures for current staffing, just as there are none for the number of service points. The most recent figures available again come from the National Consumer Council survey in 1989 which calculated that there were the equivalent to 287 full-time workers providing money advice (National Consumer Council 1990). Table 3 shows how these staff were distributed across different types of money advice service.

Table 3 Staffing of money advice services (full-time equivalent staff)

Specialist money advice centres (both independent and local authority)	68
Money advice support units	42
Money advice workers based in independent advice centres	130
Money advice workers based within local authority departments	47
	287

Source: National Consumer Council 1990

The PSI report on credit and debt, however, concluded that at least ten times as many money advisers were needed. About half a million households were identified as being in multiple debt and likely to need money advice. Earlier research had shown that one debt counsellor can cope with 100-150 cases a year, so that over 3,000 full-time equivalent staff would be needed if all the households in multiple debt sought money advice (Berthoud and Kempson 1990).

Giving money advice is a complex and highly-skilled job requiring requiring specialist training. It is not, therefore, surprising that the NCC survey showed that the bulk of money advice was provided by paid workers. Although they identified a total of 290 part-time unpaid workers they represented just 47 of the 287 full-time equivalent staff. Just about all of these unpaid workers worked in local CABx (National Consumer Council 1990).

But what scope is there for making up some of the shortfall in staffing through the use of unpaid workers? People who worked as unpaid money advisers were found to experience high levels of stress in coping with the levels of demand against the lack of resources available. They were less likely than paid staff to have received specialist training and relied on consultancy support staff. As a consequence they often felt the burden of responsibility when giving advice on subjects that could have major implications for the client if it was wrong or inadequate (Ford 1992).

While more than 8 out of 10 of unpaid money advisers found the work rewarding, over half of this group still qualified the statement with comments regarding the stress and responsibility of the work. Up to a quarter of unpaid money advice staff did not intend to continue doing such work in the foreseeable future. Indeed, the research showed a high level of turnover among unpaid staff and revealed the risk of relying on the recruitment of unpaid staff if general opportunities for paid work in the labour market improve (Ford 1992).

If adequate numbers of people could be found to work as money advisors how much more funding would money advice require? Assuming the proportion of paid workers remained the same, at 83 per cent of all full-time equivalent staff, then there would have to be the equivalent of 2,514 full-time paid workers. In its report on funding, the National Consumer Council estimated that it would cost £25,000 per year to pay, support and accommodate each paid money adviser (National Consumer Council 1992c). If we use this figure, the total costs of a comprehensive money advice service, with 2,514 full-time equivalent paid staff supported by 486 full-time equivalent volunteers, would be £63 million a year.

Support for money advisers

With such pressure on existing money advice workers it is important that they receive adequate support both to maintain the quality of advice and to relieve the burden on them through efficient systems. Recognising that need, there have been a range of national and regional developments providing consultancy support units, specialist training, specialist computer systems and information sources.

Consultancy and support units

The need for specialist money advice support units was identified in 1986 by the National Association of Citizens Advice Bureaux following the report of their Money Advice Project Group. The Group had recommended that developing a network-wide money advice service was the most appropriate way for CABx to respond to the growing demand for debt counselling. In other words, that all generalist CAB advisers should receive introductory training in debt counselling and have responsibility for delivering front-line money advice. But that they should be supported in that role by specialist skills and support which would be most efficiently located in money advice support units in each of the NACAB local areas (National Association of Citizens Advice Bureaux 1986).

Growth in this area was fairly rapid and, as we have already seen, there are currently 21 money advice support units (5 of which are directly managed by NACAB) plus another 10 agencies, like Birmingham Settlement, that combine front-line advice with consultancy and support for other local money advisers. Moreover, about a fifth of money advice funding goes towards the provision of specialist support services to advise and assist those providing money advice (Money Advice Trust 1993).

Typically these support units offer a range of services for front-line money advisers in independent advice centres or local authority departments. These include telephone helplines; highly skilled advisers who are able to take on more complex cases or representation at court hearings when needed; the provision of training and information materials, and undertaking a liaison role with local creditors (London Money Advice Support Unit 1990, Mannion 1992).

All the evidence suggests that money advice support units are highly valued by money advisers, particularly as they can take account of variations in creditor and court practices in regions across the country. There is, however, evidence that the consultancy services they offer seem to be used more by skilled money advisers than they are by the less-skilled ones they were set up to help (Mannion 1992).

Like all money advice services, the development of money advice support units has tended to be patchy and where there were private sector creditors willing to provide funding. So, although there has been an overall growth in numbers, provision is unevenly spread across the country and there are areas of high need with no support services at all. In 1990 the Money Advice Funding Working Party estimated that, to provide adequate cover nationally, 30 specialist money advice support units were required at a cost of £3 million per year (Money Advice Funding Working Party 1990).

More recently, a report to the Money Advice Trust has called for a regional structure of ten support units in England and Wales and three in Scotland. This, it proposes, should be complemented by a 'nationwide telephone consultancy service', possibly based at the Birmingham Settlement. These regional units would have a more far-reaching role than at present and 'would plan and co-ordinate at regional level all aspects of consultancy support, except certain advice provided by telephone'. It is suggested that these arrangements would attract more centralised funding from the private sector. Whether this strategy will be more efficient in fundraising and service delivery is still under consideration (Money Advice Trust 1993).

Training
In the early 1980s money advisers tended to develop their expertise by learning 'on the job' but formal training has now become firmly established for those providing money advice (National Consumer Council 1990). Indeed, the Money Advice Trust has estimated that 10 per cent of the funding of money advice is used for training. Even so, access to systematic training varies widely and is at its most extensive in the CAB service (Money Advice Trust 1993).

Responsibility for the provision of training is shared by the national co-ordinating associations, and the specialist money advice training centre at the Birmingham Settlement.

The National Money Advice Training Unit at the *Birmingham Settlement* employs two full-time trainers and one part-time, plus support staff. There is also a consultant currently attached to the unit to review the effectiveness of training provision. They offer 18 different courses ranging from a general introduction to specialist aspects of debt work, such as Dealing with distraint and Personal insolvency. Courses are run both at the Settlement and can be arranged 'off-site' for organisations that want in-house training. In 1992/3 approximately 1,000 people attended the training courses at the Settlement and a further 2,000 attended off-site courses.

While approximately 45 per cent of those attending Settlement courses come from CABx or other independent advice centres and a further 20 per cent from local authorities, there has been a gradual widening of the range of organisations using the Settlement's training facility. These include national charities and consumer credit companies who, as we have seen, are increasingly becoming involved in the direct provision of money advice, and solicitors, who are taking advantage of the Settlement's four Law Society Accredited courses available as part of the solicitors' continuing education program.

The *National Association of Citizens Advice Bureaux* provides money advice training for bureaux through its divisional training departments and money advice support units. Courses are organised both at an introductory level, for generalist advisers who may none-the-less come across people needing money advice, and at a more advanced level for those who specialise in money advice and debt work.

The *Federation of Independent Advice Centres* has recently received funding from the London Borough Grants Scheme and City Parochial Foundation to enable them to devlop introductory courses for front-line advice workers, in much the same way as NACAB does for local bureaux.

In addition there are a number of other more local courses run by money advice support units and specialist money advice centres. The Child Poverty Action Group offers a Dealing with debt three day course at Lambeth Money Advice Unit; the South Bank University and Morley College offer 'advice worker' certificate courses which include money advice modules.

In view of the wide availability of courses, the *Money Advice Association* has decided to play more of a co-ordinating role in the provision of training. Existing courses are evaluated and publicised in the Association's newsletter. Where gaps are identified the association organises specific training days taught by subject specialists. In 1994 these include courses on Taxation, Administration Orders, the Child Support Act, Debts to utility companies and Time orders. In addition to these courses, the Association runs less formal information days to raise awareness of new developments, most recently concerning the Instalment Payment Processing Facility.

The Money Advice Association has also provided input to the lead body involved in drafting standards for a National Vocational Qualification (NVQ) for advice work. The key stumbling block to this development will be finding an organisation that has the resources and credibility to assess individuals going for NVQs. It may be that a consortium of the Money Advice Association, National Association of Citizens Advice Bureaux and Federation of Independent Advice Centres will be required to fulfil this role.

But providing suitable training courses is not, it seems, sufficient to ensure that all money advisers are well-trained. A recent review for the London Advice Services Alliance identified that many advice agencies lacked specific budgets for training and that staff, as a consequence, were often unable to attend courses (Mealor 1993).

Information technology

Gathering all the information, calculating a financial statement for clients and writing standard letters to creditors is a time-consuming and complex task, but one that is repetitive and ideally suited to computerisation. Software to calculate eligibility for benefits is well established amongst advice agencies – the most commonly used package is Ferret's Helper Plus. In addition there are at least eight software packages designed for preparing the financial statements money advisers use in their negotiations with creditors. The strengths and weaknesses of each of the software packages are described in a factsheet produced by the Computer Development Unit of the London Advice Services Alliance and are summarised below:

- *DebtAlert* produced by IBM and CAS is an easy to use package that produces financial statements and standard letters. There is also the capacity for diary keeping of negotiations with creditors. It is currently used in Scotland but is being piloted by CABx in London, Lancashire and Cumbria. NACAB now has a Computer Unit for Bureaux Support that will co-ordinate and support the use of DebtAlert as standard in-house software. Although the package is very successful, NACAB do not have the capacity to train or support users outside the CAB network. .

- *DebtAdvisor* was developed by Walsall Council and ICL primarily to assist the council in the management of rent arrears. The facilities are limited and there is no storage of data after the interview.

- *DebtAssist* was developed by NACAB London Division as an interim measure before the general availability of DebtAlert. It is available to London CABx but there are no plans to extend this.

- *Ferret's DebtAid* runs on Psion Organisers and although the facilities are limited the system may be useful for advisors who do not have a personal computer and may already be using the Helper Plus software on a Psion. The fact that the organiser is small may also make it less disruptive to use during the initial interview with the client.

- *PGDebt3* was originally developed for Rugby CABx and performs the basic tasks required. However, it does not have the facilities to produce statistical reports from the database.

- *DebtAid* is generally available, is supplied free of charge and performs calculations and diary keeping of negotiations. It does not, however, create anything beyond fixed standard letters.

- *Debt Management Administration* is also generally available and has all the standard facilities. It is provided at a nominal cost but it is not possible to provide training or support which can be a major disincentive to potential users.

- The West Yorkshire Consumer Credit Counselling Service at Leeds has recently adapted debt management programme software developed in the United States. This is similar to existing packages in that it provides an assessment of the client's debts and calculates a program of debt repayment. The software will be provided as part of the support for organisations taking up WYCCCS franchises.

All the evidence shows that these packages save considerably more than the 2 per cent of adviser time they needed to save to cover their initial costs (Money Advice Trust 1993). Moreover, as most of the packages have been drawn from database software, it is usually possible to produce statistical reports from the records.

There is, then, a wide variety of software. But not all agencies have the necessary computer hardware to take advantage of it. About 70 per cent of CABx in England and Wales now have an IBM compatible computer while the figure is nearer 60 per cent amongst other independent money advisers (Money Advice Trust 1993).

There is some debate about whether computers should be used *during* the interview with the client or *after* the initial interview has been concluded. The WYCCCS bases all its debt counselling on the entry of the information into the computer and the print-out that is produced. Other money advisers are less convinced about this approach for two main reasons. First, some of them feel that keying information into a computer can disrupt an initial counselling session. Secondly, some packages are too inflexible for the variety of circumstances of clients. Trying to structure the information being given by the client to suit the program can create an even longer, and possibly off-putting, initial interview.

Finally, the variety of packages available means that there is a need to co-ordinate the development of money advice software. The information sheet on money advice software and the journal 'Computanews' produced by LASA play a crucial role in bringing together evaluations of different packages. However, as for the use of packages themselves, it seems that standardisation is only being achieved within the CABx network using DebtAlert.

Information sources
Nationally, there are three main sources of general information for advisers who may need to provide initial money advice in the course of their work: the Child Poverty Action Group *Debt advice handbook*; Birmingham Settlement's *Debt counselling handbook* and relevant sections of the NACAB Information Pack.

Specialist money advisers, however, need more detailed handbooks covering the law and procedures than can be included in a general guide. To meet this need Birmingham Settlement has published a number of guides to key areas of money advice. These publications include:

- *Homeowners and debt;*

- *An introduction to personal insolvency;*

- *Dealing with distraint;*

- *County court procedures;*

- *High court and magistrates court procedures;*

- *Self-employed and debt;*

- *Fuel debt and disrepair.*

In addition, Birmingham Settlement is currently taking part in a European Commission funded trial of a software package from the Institute for Financial Services and Consumer Protection in Hamburg.

This aims to cover all European consumer credit legislation, including case law, and details of all financial institutions in Europe. Apart from technical difficulties, experience to date suggests that there are considerable problems taking into account the diversity of laws and debt recovery practices of individual member countries.

Finally money advisers need to be kept up-to-date with developments in their field. To meet this need the Money Advice Association produces a bi-monthly newsletter, as well as regular bulletins, for those directly involved in the provision of money advice. The NACAB London Division similarly produces a bi-monthly money advice newsletter which aims to provide money advice staff with up-to-date information on case law, service developments and training opportunities. In addition, the Money Advice Association publishes a journal, *Quarterly Account*, which is aimed at broader readership of all those with an interest in money advice. This provides a forum for evaluations of different services and methods of working as well as debate about all aspects of money advice.

Summary

In excess of £3 million is spent on funding money advice services each year. Over half of this money is provided by local authorities, with the remainder coming from central government and the credit industry. Funding from the credit industry has not met expectations, with the Money Advice Trust raising less money than had been hoped.

There are about 290 full-time equivalent money advisers, most of whom are paid employees. But all the evidence suggests that comprehensive provision of money advice would require 10 times that number of advisers. If the current balance of paid and unpaid staff were maintained, and services were adequately funded, this would require an additional annual expenditure of £63 million.

With an under-resourced network of money advice centres, support services (offering consultancy, training and information) are especially important. These support services have evolved where funding was available so that access to them is uneven, creating a need for co-ordination.

4   The Use and Effectiveness of Money Advice

So far we have concentrated on aspects of the provision of money advice and debt counselling. In this chapter we turn to the use and effectiveness of these services. There are three important questions in relation to money advice services.

- How many of the people who potentially need help with debt problems do they reach?

- Which groups of people, if any, are most likely to have unmet needs for advice; and which groups are best catered for by existing advice provision?

- How effective are money advice services? Does the intervention of money advice help people in debt to improve their circumstances? Does money advice increase the likelihood of creditors being repaid the money owed to them? Does assistance from a money adviser reduce the likelihood of people facing further debt problems in the future?

The answers may be different for the different styles of money advice. If this is so, it may not be possible to identify the most effective way of providing money advice.

Levels of use of money advice
The most comprehensive information on the numbers of people seeking advice with debt problems was provided by the Policy Studies Institute study of credit and debt (Berthoud and Kempson 1992). This identified 2.5 million households in Britain and Northern Ireland who had had problem debts during 1989. That is, they had at least one commitment where they had fallen into arrears with their payments and were having difficulty repaying the money they owed. A fifth of

these, a total of half a million households across the country were in multiple debt, owing money in this way to three or more creditors.

Each of the people who were identified in this survey as having a problem debt during the previous year was asked whether they had sought any advice. Nearly 6 out of 10 of them said they had discussed their financial problems with no-one, not even their family or friends. Only a third of respondents had consulted a formal adviser, most commonly an independent money advice or debt counselling service, a solicitor or a financial adviser such as a bank manager or accountant.

Bringing these figures together, the study calculated that, at the end of 1989, there were about one million households with current problem debts who had not sought any advice. About 200,000 of these had arrears on three or more commitments and, almost by definition, could not have afforded to pay for advice. Moreover, a high proportion of them were households without bank accounts who could not have consulted a bank manager. Independent money advice services would have been the only source of help for just about all of the 200,000 multiple debt households and a significant number of the estimated 800,000 who owed money to only one or two creditors (Berthoud and Kempson 1992).

The recession which occurred shortly after the PSI survey undoubtedly increased the numbers of households who were in debt. This is shown by the rapid rise in the level of mortgage arrears and in the numbers of county court judgments for debt. Over the early 1990s banks tripled their bad debt provision and other creditors confirm informally that the debt problem worsened.

Recent reductions in the mortgage interest rate seem to have eased the situation somewhat, as has the apparent decline in unemployment. Even so, levels of debt are still not back to the 1989 figures, suggesting that the unmet need for money advice is likely, currently, to be at least one million households owing one or two creditors and plus more than a quarter of a million in multiple debt.

Who uses money advice services?
It is helpful to begin with a review of the characteristics of households who faced debt problems. Again the PSI report provides the most comprehensive picture. This study identified five characteristics which correlated with the risk of debt.

- *Age*. The younger the householder, the greater the risk of debt. Pensioners had hardly any problems.

- *Family type*. Households with children had a higher risk than those with none, and the more children there were, the greater the risk.

- *Income*. Debts were strongly related to income. Non-pensioners who had net incomes below £100 a week represented 11 per cent of all households, but accounted for 37 per cent of all debts. People who had faced a sudden drop in income were especially likely to have got into debt.

- *Commitments*. For households on moderate incomes, substantial mortgage repayments and having a number of consumer credit commitments influenced the risk of debt. Over-commitment often stemmed from a sudden drop in income.

- *Priority on payments*. Most people placed a strong priority on paying their household bills and credit commitments. But the incidence of debt was substantially higher among the minority who felt that payments could be delayed.

But what emerged from more detailed analysis was that none of these five factors led to a high risk of debt on its own. It was combinations of characteristics which led to the problem. For example, poor families without children and better-off families with children had few debts. The problems were concentrated among poor families with children.

Similar relationships existed between age and income; income and commitments; age and commitments; income and priority on payments; and age and priority on payments. But most striking of all was the analysis which looked at all five factors together. It was clear that the risk of debt was directly related to the number of pre-disposing factors reported by each household. Those who were found to be in four or five of the high risk categories had very high levels of debt. Together they accounted for 12 per cent of all households but 53 per cent of all debts. At the opposite extreme, debt was extremely rare among those who were not in any of the five high risk categories – they represented 35 per cent of all households, but accounted for only 6 per cent of all debts between them (Berthoud and Kempson 1992).

Personal circumstances

An analysis of money advice clients was carried out for the Money Advice Association shortly after the PSI survey of credit and debt and enables us to compare their characteristics with households, generally, with debt problems (Ford 1992). Data from the PSI survey of credit and debt has also been reanalysed to give a better picture of the circumstances of those who do, and do not, seek money advice.

Money advice agencies saw clients of all ages, but those aged between 25 and 34 were the largest group, accounting for 39 per cent of all users. In contrast there were far fewer younger people (aged under 25) and people aged over 55: neither group accounted for more than 10 per cent of users. Broadly speaking this mirrors the age profile of debtors as a whole, with the youngest and oldest age groups being less likely to use a money advice service. (Berthoud and Kempson 1992, Ford 1992). Much of this under-representation may be explained by a lack of awareness about money advice amongst these groups. The PSI data on credit and debt revealed that 15 per cent of those aged 29 or under did not know that they could get help with their debts. Although the figures were small, there appeared to be a similarly low level of awareness amongst pensioners.

Table 4   Comparison of family circumstances of people in debt and those who used money advice services

		column percentages
	All in debt[1]	Money advice clients[2]
Single, no children	24	26
Couple no children	14	13
Lone parent	20	14
Couples with children	36	44
Pensioners	6	2

1   Source: PSI survey of credit and debt
2   Source: Ford 1992

Turning now to type of household, we find again that the users of advice agencies were broadly similar to debtors as a whole. Overall, the largest group of money advice clients were families with children: couples with dependent children accounted for 44 per cent of all users, lone parents for a further 14 per cent. But, while lone parents were under-represented, there were more couples with dependent children among the money advice clients than among debtors as a whole (Berthoud and Kempson 1992, Ford 1992). We can only speculate about the reasons for this apparent discrepancy.

An earlier study of money advice services showed that many people had found it hard to confront the fact that they were in financial difficulty. Among couples, one of them typically assumed responsibility for bill-paying and this person often hid the difficulties from the partner, feeling that he or she had let the family down by getting into arrears (Hinton and Berthoud 1988). If this were true then we would expect couples to be *less* not *more* likely to seek help. An alternative explanation might be that debt was so common among lone parents – half of them had problem debts – that it was seen as a fact of life (Berthoud and Kempson 1992). In other words fatalism might have led them to put up with their lot.

Tenure

The analysis by housing tenure lends further support to this second explanation. The earlier study of credit and debt showed that a quarter of council tenants had problem debts, five times the proportion of owner-occupiers (Berthoud and Kempson 1992).

Owner-occupiers had sought help with debt problems from a broad range of financial advisers. The PSI study of credit and debt found that 16 per cent of home-owners in debt had consulted a bank manager or accountant for money advice, compared with only 1 per cent of tenants. Council tenants were especially likely to have said they contacted either an independent advice agency or a local office of the Department of Social Security (Berthoud and Kempson 1992).

A study of citizens advice bureaux in the traditionally affluent South East, which was also carried out at the end of the 1980s, revealed a changing picture of clients asking for money advice. An increasing number of home-owners, often with very high mortgage commitments, were seeking help having been made redundant (National Association of Citizens Advice Bureaux 1988). The analysis of money advice clients in 1992 shows that this trend continued into the early 1990s (Table 5).

While the level of mortgage arrears rose substantially between the fieldwork for the PSI study and the analysis of money advice clients,

Table 5 Comparison of tenure of people in debt and those who used money advice services

Column percentages

	All in debt[1]	Money advice clients[2]	NACAB[3]
Owner occupiers	30	49	41
Social tenants	55	39	40
Private sector tenants	12	12	19

1   Source: PSI survey of credit and debt
2   Source: Ford 1992
3   Source: Walker 1990 (figures are based on an average of 17 local bureaux records)

this rise alone is insufficient to account for the fact that owner-occupiers out-numbered council tenants among the householders who had consulted a money adviser (Ford 1992).

Economic circumstances
There were also interesting differences in levels of economic activity between people in debt and those who consulted money advice services. Unemployed people were over-represented amongst those who had consulted a money adviser, while people in work and those who were retired were under-represented.

Given this finding, it is interesting to look at the economic circumstances of users of the West Yorkshire Consumer Credit Counselling Service. The WYCCCS, as we have seen, was set up to meet the needs of people with sufficient disposable income to set up repayment plans with their creditors in a higher proportion than other forms of money advice service. Although we do not have information about the economic activity of their clients, we do have details of their incomes. On average, people who consulted the WYCCCS had incomes of £1,196 a month. This is twice the income (£602) of households with three or more debts in the survey of credit and debt. Even allowing for inflation since the credit and debt survey, users of the WYCCCS are likely to be a great deal better-off than multiple debtors as a whole and users of other money advice services in particular (Smith 1994).

Table 6   Comparison of economic activity of people in debt and those who used money advice services

Column percentages

	All in debt[1]	Money advice clients[2]
Employee	51	43
Self-employed	8	6
Unemployed	5	26
Retired, sick or disabled	29	12
Home-maker or carer	6	10
Student	1	2

1   Source: PSI survey of credit and debt
2   Source: Ford 1992

Extent of debt

As we have already seen, the great majority of people in debt owed money to only one creditor, while it was quite clear that money advisers were predominantly seeing people in multiple debt. People who owed money to just one creditor were greatly under-represented among money advice clients, while those who were in arrears with four or more commitments were over-represented by a similar margin (Berthoud and Kempson 1992, Ford 1992).

Table 7   Comparison of the number of arrears of people in debt and those who used money advice services

Column percentages

	All in debt[1]	Money advice clients[2]
Arrears on 1 commitment	55	15
Arrears on 2 commitments	22	11
Arrears on 3 commitments	10	11
Arrears on 4 or more commitments	12	63

1   Source: PSI survey of credit and debt
2   Source: Ford 1992

Reanalysis of the PSI credit and debt survey data showed that while only 7 per cent of those with arrears on one commitment had sought advice from either a general advice agency or specialist money advisor, 16 per cent of those with four or more commitments in arrears had done so.

It is a frequent complaint from money advisers that they see people too late, when they are already in multiple debt. As a consequence, it takes many hours to sort out their finances and set up repayment schedules with their creditors. These figures demonstrate that situation all too clearly. It is further confirmed by the NACAB review of money advice clients, in which Staffordshire CABx reported that 52 per cent of clients had sought advice only after court action had been taken against them. Very often it was only something as drastic as a court summons that had triggered individuals to begin facing up to the fact that they had financial difficulties and needed to seek help (Walker 1990).

There are, however, a number of possible explanations of this finding. As we have already seen, many people cannot face up to the fact that they have got into financial difficulties until things have really got out of hand (Hinton and Berthoud 1988). Even when people acknowledge that they are in serious financial difficulty they may feel strongly that it is a personal matter that they must sort out in private. This reluctance to let others know your business was the most frequent explanation given by those in the PSI study of credit and debt who had not sought help.

At the same time, however, it seems very likely that some people dip into arrears but manage to repay the money they owe and avoid multiple debt. These people would be unlikely to need the assistance of a money adviser and would naturally be under-represented among the clients of money advice services. In fact, people with only one debt were most likely to consider it a temporary stage that they had the resources to overcome. Of those with one problem debt who had not sought advice, 1 in 10 gave this as the reason. None of the people with four or more debts did so (Berthoud and Kempson 1992).

Telephone helplines were developed in an attempt to address the perceived problem of people delaying seeking advice. It is interesting, therefore, to note that although the report on a caller survey of the National Debtline claims that people had contacted them when they were only a few months behind with payments, it also records that 'the majority of those replying to the questionnaire identified between three and five debts' (National Debtline 1992).

Types of debt

The PSI study of credit and debt showed that debts on household bills were far more common than arrears on consumer credit commitments. Moreover, it identified a clear link between the nature of the debts and the sources of help people turned to.

Three-quarters of those seeking advice about arrears on consumer credit commitments had consulted an independent advice agency such as a money advice service or citizens advice bureau. The one exception to this was people who had problem overdrafts, most of whom had been in contact with their bank manager. In contrast, people with debts on household bills had sought advice from a much wider range of organisations, including solicitors and social workers. Even so, 4 out of 10 of enquiries about debts on household bills had been made at independent advice services (Berthoud and Kempson 1992).

Comparison between money advice clients and debtors as a whole confirms this analysis. It was clear that money advice services had seen a disproportionate number of clients with consumer credit arrears, especially those in difficulties with the repayments on plastic cards and loans (Table 8).

Table 8   Comparison of the extent of arrears on consumer credit commitments of people in debt and those who used money advice services

		Percentages
	All in debt[1]	Money advice clients[2]
Overdraft	20	18
Credit/store card	12	28
Bank/building soc.loan	10	23
Finance house loan	*	18
HP/credit sale	10	15
Mail order	11	12
Moneylender/check trader	*	5

1   Source: PSI survey of credit and debt
2   Source: Ford 1992

An in-depth study of money advice clients at the Birmingham Settlement revealed a similarly high level of consumer credit arrears.

Out of the 26 clients interviewed, 22 were in difficulty with a consumer creditor (Jones, Wainwright and Doling 1993). In contrast the proportion of money advice clients with debts on most household bills was at about the level that might be expected from the overall picture of debt, with the main exception of of rent and mortgage arrears (Table 9).

Table 9   Comparison of the extent of arrears on household bills of people in debt and those who used money advice services

Percentages

	All in debt[1]	Money advice clients[2]
Rent	43	18
Mortgage	12	26
Community charge	19	47
Water rates	14	20
Gas	15	14
Electricity	16	13
Telephone	4	12
Income tax	3	7
Fines	4	4

1   Source: PSI survey of credit and debt

2   Source: Ford 1992

There are two possible explanations for the under-representation of rent arrears and the higher than expected mortgage arrears among money advice clients. Earlier analysis of debt suggested that rent arrears commonly occurred in households that were up-to-date with their other commitments, while mortgage arrears most often occurred in households who were in multiple debt. And, as we have seen, multiple debtors were much more numerous among money advice clients. At the same time it was clear that rent arrears tended to be clustered in particular localities, lending further support to the earlier hypothesis that people living in communities where debt was common-place might have been more fatalistic about their situation and less inclined to seek advice (Berthoud and Kempson 1992, Kempson 1994).

How effective are money advice services?
There are three broad criteria against which money advice services can be assessed:

- from the debtors' viewpoint, the extent to which financial stability is restored and hardship is avoided or alleviated;

- from the creditors' point of view, whether and how quickly the arrears are repaid;

- and, more generally, whether the involvement of a money adviser reduces the likelihood of a household getting into difficulties again in the future.

Relatively few studies have looked in detail at effectiveness and this is an area where more research is clearly needed. It is, however, possible to begin a tentative assessment from existing data.

The debtors' viewpoint
The most concrete way in which people in debt can be helped is by increasing their income so that they have more money to repay their creditors. Indeed this is usually one of the first steps taken by a money adviser. Here there is very clear evidence of the benefit of money advice to debtors. An in-depth study of 26 people who had received help from a money advice centre showed that money advisers had initiated a total of 52 claims for additional welfare benefits (Hinton and Berthoud 1988). In addition, a number of reports give details of the percentage of money advice clients who were helped to increase their income. They include:

- 87 per cent of users of the Bradford Debt Counselling Unit (Bradford DCU 1985);

- 71 per cent of users of the Leicestershire Money Advice Centre (Leicester MAC 1985);

- 50 per cent of the CAB Debt Counselling Unit (National Association of Citizens Advice Bureaux 1983);

- 43 per cent of users of the Birmingham Court Duty Welfare Officer (Davies 1982).

Secondly, money advice can assist clients by restoring a degree of order to their financial affairs. Typically money advisers prepare (or help the client to prepare) a statement of income and expenditure, from which they calculate a realistic repayment schedule for all the creditors owed money. A survey of National Debtline users shcwed that 95 per cent were subsequently able to negotiate repayment plans with their creditors, although in 7 out of 10 cases they had succeeded with only a proportion of their creditors in the first instance. Three-quarters of all users said that they had eventually been able to make affordable arrangements to repay the money they owed (National Debtline 1992).

The recently-established West Yorkshire Consumer Credit Counselling Service took 1,000 initial enquiries in the first nine months of operation. 'Debt managment programmes', where clients made one monthly payment to the WYCCCS which allocated this money to the various creditors, were set up for 180 of the eventual clients (Smith 1993).

On a smaller scale, an in-depth study of money advice clients showed that satisfactory repayment schedules were much more likely following the intervention of a money adviser. Sixteen cases were studied in detail, of which only three people already had satisfactory schedules before they contacted a money adviser, but a further six had set them up after seeking help from the money advice centre (Hinton and Berthoud 1988).

A later depth interview survey of 15 money advice clients showed that 12 had been helped to reduce or reschedule the repayments to their creditors, 10 had interest suspended on the balance outstanding and one had debts written off. Some clients had noticed a change in creditors' attitudes so that they were more able reach an agreement with the help of the money adviser (Mannion 1992).

Many people fail to contact a money advice centre until they face court proceedings by their creditor, repossession of their home, disconnection of their fuel or water supply or business failure. The third main benefit of money advice from the debtors' point of view is help in averting such imminent crises.

A survey of 542 housing possession cases showed that very few people were represented at the court hearing, but when they were the likelihood of a possession order being granted was reduced from 22 per cent to 4 per cent (Watts 1987).

Again, the two depth interview surveys provide useful information on the outcomes of money advice. The Policy Studies Institute research showed that 18 of the 26 people had faced homelessness when they contacted the money advice centre. In all cases this was averted. In addition, 20 of the people had debts to other creditors who were threatening court action or disconnection of utilities. The report notes that:

> *We cannot be certain what would have happened to the 42 priority debts in the absence of money advice, but the success of the technique is at least indicated by the fact that none of the clients interviewed was evicted, disconnected, distrained or imprisoned during their course of intensive assistance (Hinton and Berthoud 1988).*

The later study, of 15 money advice clients, found that nine people had imminent court proceedings against them stopped by the money adviser; two retained goods that were about to be repossessed; two avoided losing their homes and one person's electricity supply was retained (Mannion 1992).

Users of money advice services found such crisis intervention the most valuable aspect of the work of the money adviser. People who had used Birmingham Settlement money advice centre consistently stated that they could never have managed without their help (Jones, Wainwright and Doling 1993).

A report on the first 15 months of Business Debtline shows a high level of success in avoiding small business failure. Of the people who had consulted them, 85 per cent were able to continue trading, even though most had been on the brink of going out of business at the time they contacted the service. This compared very favourably with local levels of small business failure. The local Training and Enterprise Council estimated that about a third of new businesses had ceased to trade within a year and a half; two-thirds within five years. There was a similar level of achievement with averting possession proceedings. At the time they consulted Business Debtline 98 out of the 413 users had possessions proceedings against their home either started or threatened. Only nine people subsequently went on to lose their home (Business Debtline 1994).

Although the evidence is less quantifiable, it is quite apparent that money advice clients experienced substantial benefit from the relief of stress and worry. Several of the reports quote the words of users:

> *I think I would have been in mental hospital by now ... I can sleep better now (Hinton and Berthoud 1988).*

> *... in myself I'm not well -- but at least a lot of the worry is lifted. I'm a lot better than I was, I was crying all the time, taking pills you know (Mannion 1992).*

We're not arguing any more ... it has taken the strain off (Mannion 1992).

The service has taken a weight off our minds (Smith 1993).

Without people like you, people like me would commit suicide (Smith 1993).

... we have been given the incentive, encouragement and motivation to continue and plan for recovery when all was looking black around us (Business Debtline 1994).

But a survey of clients of the Birmingham Settlement money advice centre showed that, after the initial relief, they often became anxious if there was a long period of negotiation between the money advisor and creditors. Some clients, if they had not heard regularly from the advisor during this period, had decided to act independently and on occasion went against the advice they had been given (Jones, Wainwright and Doling 1993).

The creditors' viewpoint
Taken together, then, there was a good deal of evidence of the benefits of money advice from the debtors' point of view. The same was not necessarily so for creditors.

Of course, any intervention that results in debtors increasing their income must eventually lead to some benefit for their creditors. But the key concern of creditors is likely to be whether the people owing money to them are helped to set up and adhere to realistic repayment agreements. Here the available evidence seems equivocal.

Three studies have attempted to measure the effects of money advice on the repayment of debts: the two depth interview surveys of money advice clients and a study of administration orders.

The Policy Studies Institute research included discussion of 16 individual cases with creditors. Only three of these 16 debts were judged by creditors to have satisfactory repayment schedules before the intervention of the money adviser, while the remaining 13 had a history of missed payments. In seven cases there had been a series of arrangements that turned out to be unrealistic and had been broken. Following the involvement of money advisers, the number of clients judged by the creditor to have satisfactory repayment agreements had increased from three to nine; a further four had a series of missed payments, but the money advice agency was able to negotiate a new arrangement and in only three cases had the arrangements broken down altogether (Hinton and Berthoud 1988).

The study of administration orders also seemed to suggest that the involvement of a money adviser led to more regular debt payment and to larger sums of money being repaid to creditors. (Administration orders are set up by courts for debtors with a court judgment entered against them, and allow for a single payment to be paid to the court, which then distributes the money pro-rata to all·creditors.) After two years, three-quarters of administration orders set up by money advisers were up-to-date, compared with just a quarter of those where there was no money advice involvement. This difference was not quite so marked after four years, but even so orders were twice as likely to be up-to-date where a money adviser had been involved (65 per cent, compared with 33 per cent) (Davies 1986).

The most recent study, however, suggested that there were considerable variations in the success of negotiated repayment schedules with different creditors. While repayment of rent arrears was improved by the involvement of a money adviser, the same was not true for arrears owed to a retail creditor, a bank or a utility company (Mannion 1992).

Eighteen months after repayment schedules had been negotiated for rent arrears, 10 per cent of tenants who had consulted a money adviser had repaid their arrears in full, five times the proportion of a control group who had not sought advice. Among those who still had rent arrears, the money advice clients, on average, owed substantially less than the control group – £1,262 compared with £2,031 – although it must be noted that even the money advice clients' rent arrears had increased slightly over this period (Mannion 1992).

In contrast, money advice seemed to make little difference to the levels and regularity of debt repayment to either a retail creditor or a bank. There was some indication that money advice clients may have been slightly more likely to clear their debts altogether, but this has to be balanced by a larger number having their debts written off (Mannion 1992).

The picture for fuel debt was different again. While it was clear that money advice clients had not, as a group, repaid more of the money they owed than a control group who had not sought advice, they did seem to have been more successful at keeping to negotiated repayment plans (Mannion 1992).

So, the evidence on levels of repayment appears contradictory but, as the numbers of cases involved in the studies was not large, the findings must be treated with a degree of caution.

At the same time, there was evidence that the intervention of money advisers may have reduced the costs to creditors of recovering the money owed to them. It was clear that contact with a money adviser led creditors to modify their debt recovery actions (Hinton and Berthoud 1988, Mannion 1992).

The long-term influences of money advice

To be effective, money advice should, ideally, reduce the likelihood of further debt problems in the long term. And it is here that the evidence is even thinner on the ground, as studies tend to focus on money advice clients at the outset of the process. Such information as we have relates to one-to-one counselling and suggests that debtors found it difficult to maintain repayment schedules and that initial enthusiasm for the help provided by money advisers began to wane after about six to nine months (Hinton and Berthoud 1988, Mannion 1992, Jones, Wainwright and Doling 1993).

Follow up interviews conducted with clients of the Birmingham Money Advice Centre showed that, after the early relief of finding help, clients were surprised at how long it would take to pay off the debts, indeed some schedules stretched beyond the client's lifetime (Jones, Wainwright and Doling 1993).

Even so, as we have just seen, money advice clients more frequently kept up with their repayments than those who had not sought advice. But keeping to a budget that was normally even tighter than before seeking advice was extremely difficult. Some clients were regularly going without holidays, clothes, shoes and even food in order to keep to their repayment schedules (Hinton and Berthoud 1988).

There was also evidence that people differed in the degree to which they had acquired the skills to handle their own financial affairs, having consulted a debt counsellor. Some clearly felt better equipped to deal with debt problems in the future.

The client said that the most important thing about going to the money advice centre has been that they had the knowledge to know what to do. They knew about adminstration orders and how to get them. She said that there was no way she could have done this by herself (Jones, Wainwright and Doling 1993).

But, for other clients, this form of intensive intervention ran the risk of creating a climate of dependency on the money adviser and some people returned to the money advice centre with every new financial hurdle that arose (Jones, Wainwright and Doling 1993).

Which is the most cost effective way of delivering money advice?
Few people now question the need for money advice. Even if the benefits to creditors are unproven, there is much less doubt about the value of money advice for people who find themselves in debt. But the question that creditors and money advisers alike want answered is *which is the most cost-effective way of delivering money advice?*

As we have already seen, there is a wide variety of styles of money advice. These range in cost from initial advice plus self-help packs which are designed to enable the debtor to negotiate unassisted with creditors (National Debtline, for example), to advisers who negotiate with creditors but leave maintenance of repayments to the debtor (the usual approach of voluntary sector money advisers), to services such as the West Yorkshire Consumer Credit Counselling Service that both negotiates and manages repayment schedules on behalf of the client.

Added to this, some services tend to attract clients at an earlier stage in the debt cycle than do others, with a greater likelihood of getting the debts repaid quickly. Outreach money advice services, operated by local authorities and independent advice agencies, establish contact with clients when they owe money to just one or two creditors (Kempson 1987). At the other extreme, court-based money advisers or those who participate in duty rota schemes, by definition, see people who have become involved in litigation (Watts 1987).

Comparing the costs and effectiveness of these different approaches is the most significant gap in the research to date.

Commonsense would seem to suggest that less time will be needed to negotiate with creditors and likely outcome improved the earlier contact is established with potential clients. But the costs of outreach work cannot be ignored.

Similarly, money advice services that assist clients to negotiate with their creditors themselves will be cheaper to run than those that undertake the negotiations on their clients' behalf, especially if they also manage their repayment schedules. If, however, money advice clients prove unable to negotiate successful repayment plans, services adopting a self-help approach will be less effective than those undertaking case-work.

So, what is the evidence? It is in this area that evidence is especially thin on the ground and there are no comparative studies at all.

A survey of callers to National Debtline showed that 82 per cent had been able to work out a personal budget and 75 per cent of them had been able to set up repayment plans with their creditors that they felt they could afford. About half of them had succeeded in either reducing their mortgage or rent arrears (29 per cent) or had cleared the arrears altogether (20 per cent). In a quarter of cases the amount owed was unchanged, while a quarter had mounting rent or mortgage arrears. Similarly 4 out of 10 had managed to repay their other creditors in full. About eight out of ten clients felt that it was the self-help booklet, rather than telephone advisers, that helped them with these successful outcomes (National Debtline 1992). This seems to suggest that a self-help approach can be successful, at least in the short-term, for a significant number of people. But it clearly has its limitations.

Clients of face-to-face counselling may not feel so able to take the same level of control over their financial affairs if the adviser takes the lead in the negotiation with creditors. A separate study of 26 clients at the Birmingham Money Advice Centre found that after the initial interview the clients

> *... did not appear to see themselves as active participants in the process, or at least a clear role for the client did not come over as having been established within the course of the interview (Jones, Wainwright and Doling 1993).*

Summary

There is a considerable level of unmet need for money advice and debt counselling. This may amount to as many as a million people a year. Lone parents, council tenants, and people who were either in employment or were economically inactive were all under-represented among the users of money advice services compared with the number who were in debt.

The users of money advice centres were drawn disproportionately from those facing multiple debt and people in arrears with consumer credit commitments or mortgages. Many were in quite serious difficulties by the time they sought advice.

There was clear evidence of the benefit of money advice from the debtors' viewpoint, with people being helped to negotiate repayment schedules with their creditors and avoid debt enforcement proceedings. Levels of stress and worry were correspondingly reduced, but there was some indication that, after this initial relief, people became anxious if negotiations with creditors became prolonged.

In contrast, the evidence of the benefits to creditors was rather more equivocal. Overall, it seems that the intervention of a money adviser increased the likelihood of arrears being repaid, but there were considerable differences between creditors in the success rates of negotiated repayment plans.

The long-term effects of money advice intervention were even less clear-cut, and seemed likely to vary between the different styles of service delivery. More research is required before we can say with any confidence how money advice can be delivered most cost-effectively.

5 The Future of Money Advice

Money advice is a well-established feature of social provision in Britain. Indeed it is the envy of most other countries, not just in terms of the extent but the variety of provision and the skills of those who work as money advisers.

But we cannot ignore the big shortfalls in provision, either measured against levels of multiple debt or in terms of the pressures being placed on existing services. By both measures there needs to be a substantial development in services – perhaps as much as a tenfold increase in existing staffing levels at a total annual cost of £63 million. Although this is a large sum of money, it pales into insignificance against either the estimated £1 billion owed in arrears (Berthoud and Kempson 1992) or the £53 billion outstanding in consumer credit agreements (Central Statistical Office 1994).

The key questions for the future are: how should the expansion in money advice services be funded? what is the most effective way of delivering services? and how should they be co-ordinated?

Funding

The National Consumer Council report offers the clearest way forward. They conclude that the credit industry *should* bear some of the cost. While the proposed network of Consumer Credit Counselling Services would fulfil *part* of this responsibility, such services will inevitably concentrate on helping people with sufficient income to make substantial offers to repay their creditors. The industry responsibility, however, should be wider than this and encompass people who, through no fault of their own, suffer drops in income that leave them seriously over-committed (National Consumer Council 1992c).

All the signs are that, with notable exceptions, the credit industry seems unlikely voluntarily to provide the sort of funding needed. The

National Consumer Council proposes that central government (they suggest the Department of Trade and Industry) should take the lead in encouraging the private sector to fund money advice services. This recommendation was made at a time when the credit industry was going through the worst slump it has, perhaps, ever seen. As the industry begins to emerge from these difficulties it may be time to look again at the National Consumer Council proposals.

At the same time, it is important not to lose sight of the problems associated with the insecurity of funding from local and central government. A high proportion of people using money advice services (and indeed those in multiple debt) are living on state benefits and owe money on basic household bills rather than consumer credit commitments. Again the National Consumer Council report is useful in pointing the way forward. They recommend that:

> *The Department of the Environment, the Scottish Office and the Welsh Office should ensure local authorities are able to continue to fund money advice services at a local level by recognising the funding commitments through central grant allocation (National Consumer Council 1992c).*

Assessing the effectiveness of different methods of service delivery

Perhaps our second question is the one that needs answering more urgently. We have reached the situation where money advice is provided through a wide range of organisations, which employ a diversity of ways of delivering money advice with widely differing costs of delivery. Indeed this diversity is the strength of money advice provision in Britain, but which method of service delivery is the most effective and where should the balance of development lie in the future?

The Money Advice Trust commissioned a report to address this question, primarily by canvassing current opinion. Useful as this is, it really needs to be complemented, as the National Consumer Council identified, by research to assess the cost-effectiveness of different styles of work. Only then can we begin to answer key questions like:

- How many people can, with help, sort out their own financial problems and negotiate with their creditors themselves?

- How many people will need one-to-one debt counselling and, of these, how many have sufficient income to make a cost-recovery service (like the West Yorkshire Consumer Credit Counselling Service) viable?

- How do we ensure that people use money advice services *before* they get into serious difficulties, either by encouraging them to contact services earlier or by the services themselves seeking out people who are getting into financial difficulties?

Co-ordination

The final point that needs to be addressed concerns the co-ordination of money advice services. The credit industry tends towards a corporatist view and feels that there should be a far greater degree of co-ordination between services than exists at present. But organisations that run money advice services are not subsidiaries of a parent company. Indeed it is hard to see how such co-ordination could be brought about when some services are provided directly by local authorities and some operate as independent agencies.

The situation is further complicated by the existence of different systems of franchises. In many ways the National Association of Citizens Advice Bureaux offers franchises to advice centres that wish to operate as a CAB. The proposals for expanding the network of Consumer Credit Counselling Services and Business Debtline are also to be franchise-based. Any move by the credit industry to link future funding of money advice to co-ordination of services seems somewhat unrealistic under these circumstances.

A more fruitful and realistic approach seems to lie in developing a closer collaboration between organisations and for the diversity of provision to be accepted as a strength rather than a weakness.

Bibliography

Bassano A, 'Instalment Payment Plan Facility (IPPF)', *Quarterly Account*, 29, Autumn 1993, pp 6-7

Berthoud R and Kempson E, *Credit and Debt, The PSI Report*, Policy Studies Institute, 1992

Brady A and O'Brien J, *Directory of Debt and Money Advice*, University of the West of England, 1994

Business Debtline, *Progress Report for Business Debtline's Advisory Group*, January 1994

Central Statistical Office, *Social Trends 24, 1994 Edition*, HMSO, 1994

Conlin J, 'The missing link', *Consumer Credit Association News*, 15(1), January 1994, pp 12-13

Consumer Credit Association, 'A solution with dignity', *Consumer Credit Association News*, 15(1), January 1994, pp 7-11

Davies J, 'Delegalisation of debt recovery proceedings: a socio-legal study of money advice centres and administration orders', in Ramsay I (ed), *Creditors and Debtors*, Professional Books, 1986

Ford J, *The Characteristics and Circumstances of Money Advice Clients*, Report to the Nuffield Foundation, 1992

Ford J, *The Role of Volunteer Money Advisors,* Joseph Rowntree Foundation Findings, 1992.

Greater Manchester/East Cheshire Money Advice Project, *Dealing with Debt: a report on the first year's progress of the Greater Manchester/East Cheshire Money Advice Project,* National Association of Citizens Advice Bureaux, 1989

Hartropp A et al, *Families in Debt,* Jubilee Centre Publications, 1988

Hinton T and Berthoud R, *Money Advice Services,* Policy Studies Institute, 1988

Johnson S, 'Money advice helplines, self-help or no help?', *Quarterly Account*, 29, Autumn 1993, pp 12-13

Jones N, Wainwright S and Doling J, *Money Advice, Users' Experience*, University of Birmingham, Department of Social Policy, 1993

Kempson E, *Advice and Law Centres in Redditch,* Acumen, 1987

Kempson E, *Debt Recovery and Money Advice: their costs, benefits and effectiveness,* Acumen, 1988

Legal aid: *42nd Annual Report of the Law Society and the Lord Chancellor's Advisory Committee* (1992-3)

London Money Advice Support Unit, *Debt in London*, The Greater London CAB Service, 1990

London Money Advice Support Unit, 'The "Leeds" Project', *Money Advice Newsletter*, 20, February/March 1993, p 3

Mannion R, *Dealing with Debt: an evaluation of money advice services,* HMSO, 1992

Mealor G, *Money Advice, Training Development in the Voluntary Sector,* London Advice Services Alliance, 1993

Money Advice Association, *Annual Report 1991-2,* 1992

Money Advice Funding Working Party, *Report of the Money Advice Funding Working Party*, 1990

Money Advice Scotland, *Directory of Money Advice Services in Scotland*, MAS, 1991

Money Advice Trust, *Support for Money Advice: Next Steps*, Money Advice Trust, 1993

National Association of Citizens Advice Bureaux, *Report of the Money Advice Project Group*, NACAB, 1986

National Association of Citizens Advice Bureaux, South East Area Money Advice Support Unit, *Debt Problems in Kent and East Sussex*, NACAB, 1988

National Consumer Council, *The Fourth Right of Citizenship: a review of local advice services*, NCC, 1977

National Consumer Council, *Money Advice, Debt Counselling and Money Advice Services Training and Publications: a summary*, NCC, 1982

National Consumer Council, *Consumers and Debt,* NCC, 1983

National Consumer Council, *Debt Advice Provision in the UK,* NCC, 1990

National Consumer Council, *Court Without Advice: duty court-based advice and representation schemes,* NCC, 1992a

National Consumer Council, *Funding Money Advice Services: a statutory levy on the credit industry: the options,* NCC, 1992b

National Consumer Council, *Money Advice Services: final report and recommendations for funding,* NCC, 1992c

National Debtline, *Caller Survey*, Birmingham Settlement, 1992

National Debtline, *Dealing With Your Debts: advice on debt problems for people with mortgages*, Birmingham Settlement, 1993a

National Debtline, *Dealing With Your Debts: advice on debt problems for people who pay rent*, Birmingham Settlement, 1993b

Parker, G, 'Indebtedness', in Walker R and Parker G (eds), *Money Matters,* Sage, 1988

Smith H, *Client Satisfaction Survey*, West Yorkshire Consumer Credit Counselling Service, 1993

Stephens, B, *The Finance Industry and Money Advice, Committed or not?*, National Association of Citizens Advice Bureaux, 1989

Wainwright S, Ford J and Doling J, 'Money advice issues for local authorities', *Local Government Studies*, 18 (3), Autumn 1992, pp 249-259

Walker T, *Debt and Money Advice, The CABx Experience*, National Association of Citizens Advice Bureaux, 1990

Wann, M, *An Evaluation of the NACAB Self-Help Booklets 'Dealing with Your Debts'*, July 1993, National Association of Citizens Advice Bureaux, 1993

Wann, M, *Evaluation of the Booklets 'Dealing with Your Debts'*, May 1994, National Association of Citizens Advice Bureaux, 1994

Watts J, 'Local authority possession proceedings', *Legal Action*, February 1987, pp 6-7

Woolfe M and Ivison J, *Debt Advice Handbook*, Child Poverty Action Group, 1994